I'm not trying to be sexy. It's just my way of expressing myself when I move around.

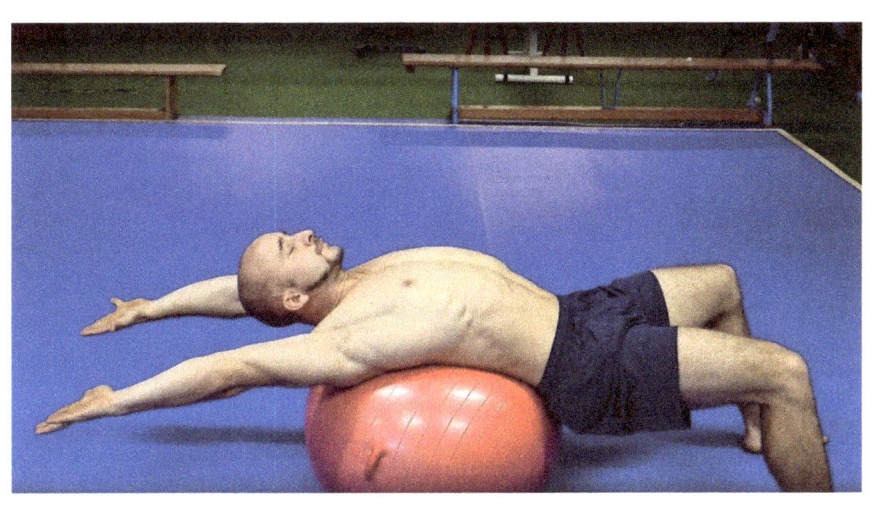

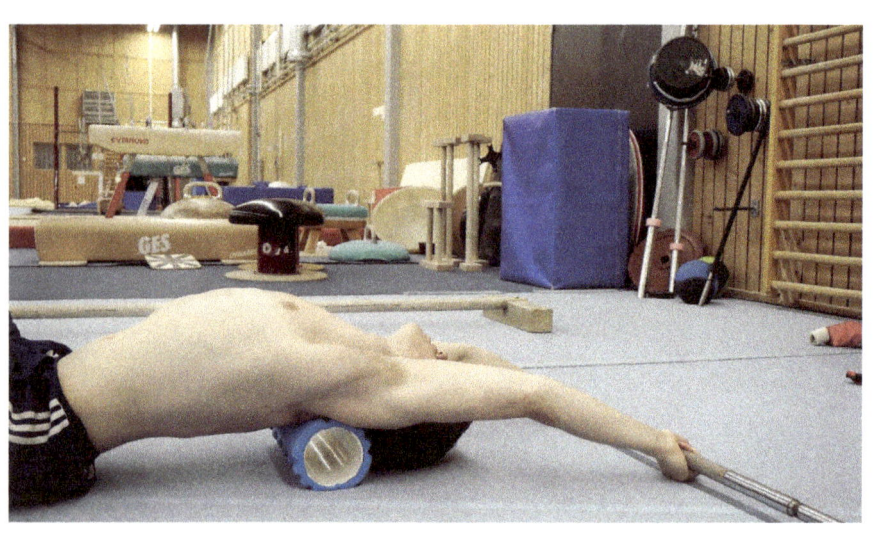

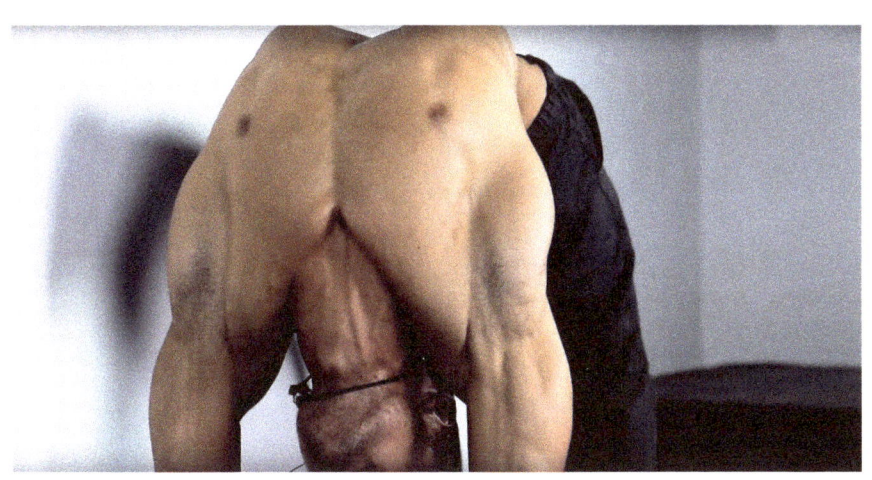

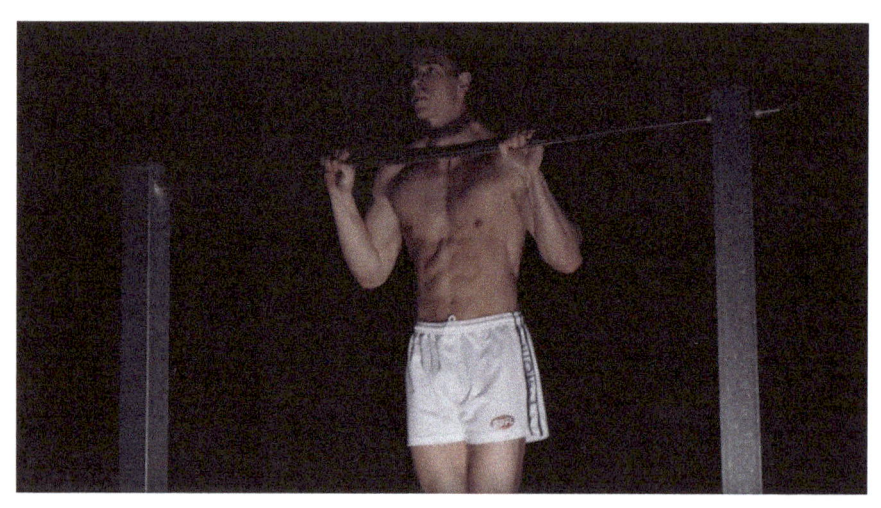

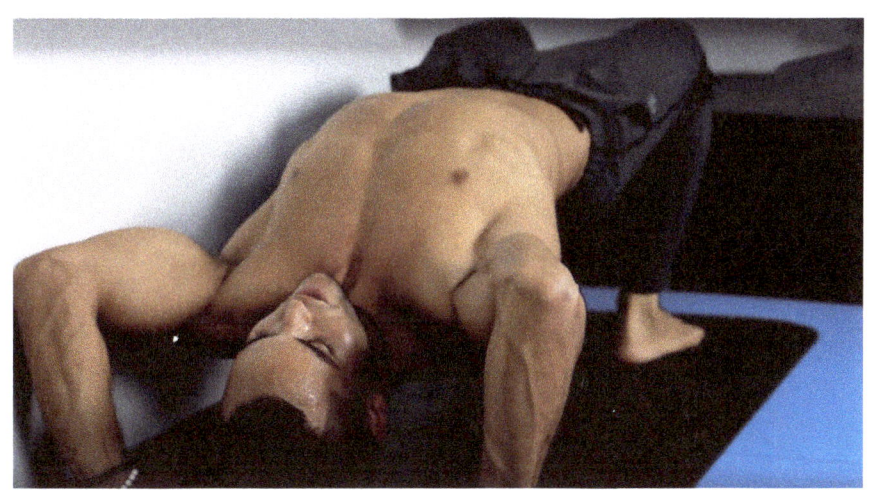

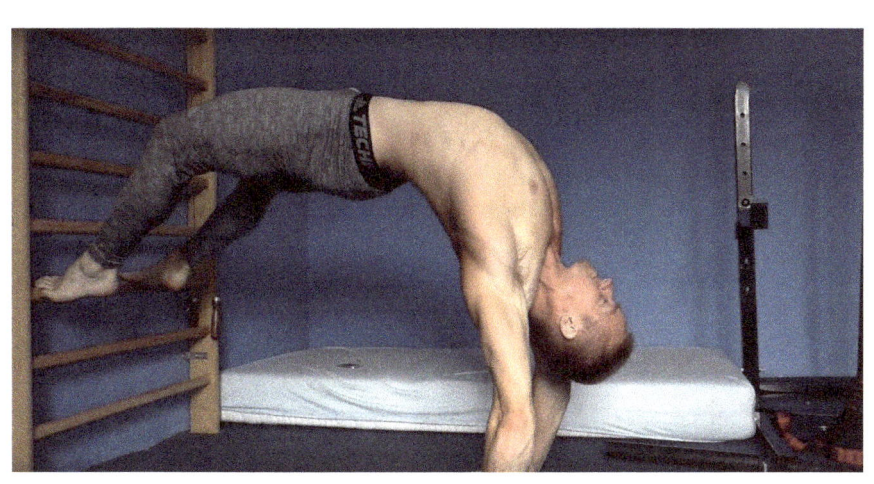

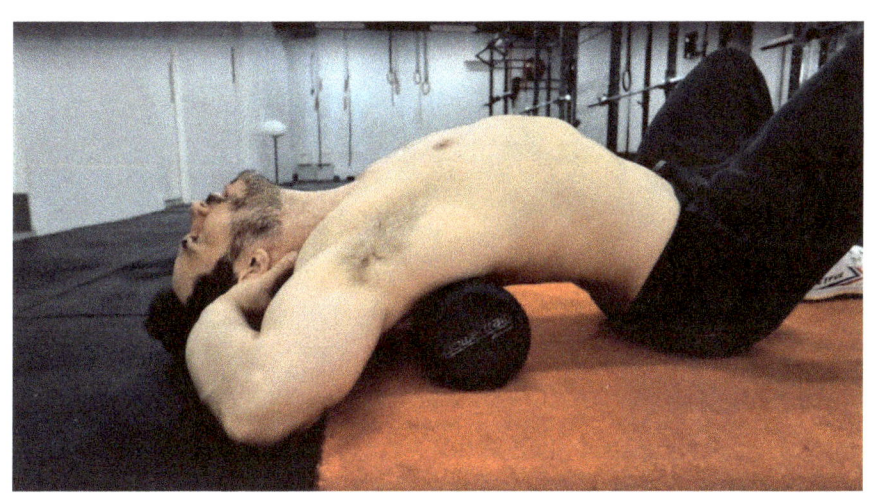

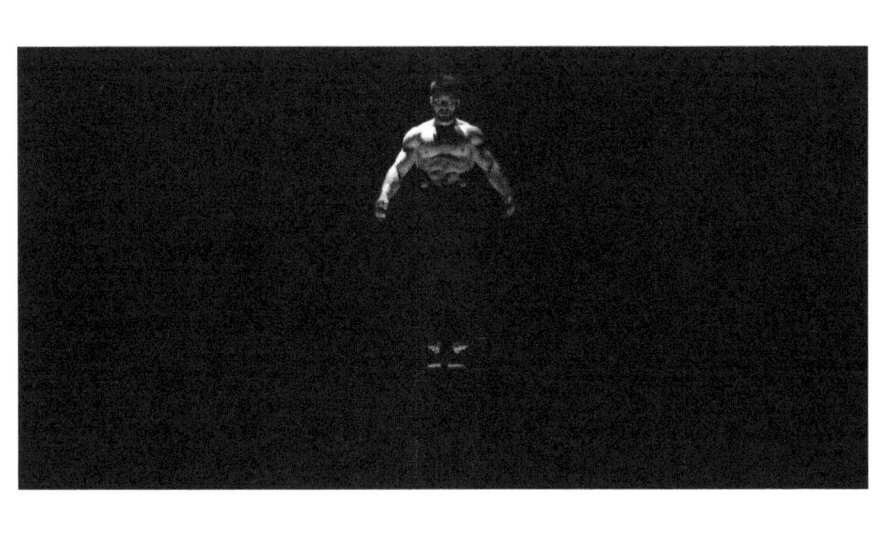

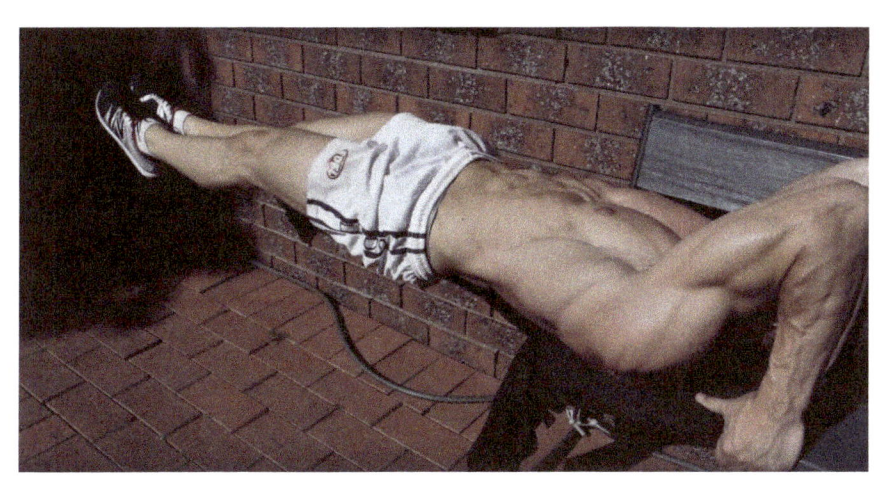

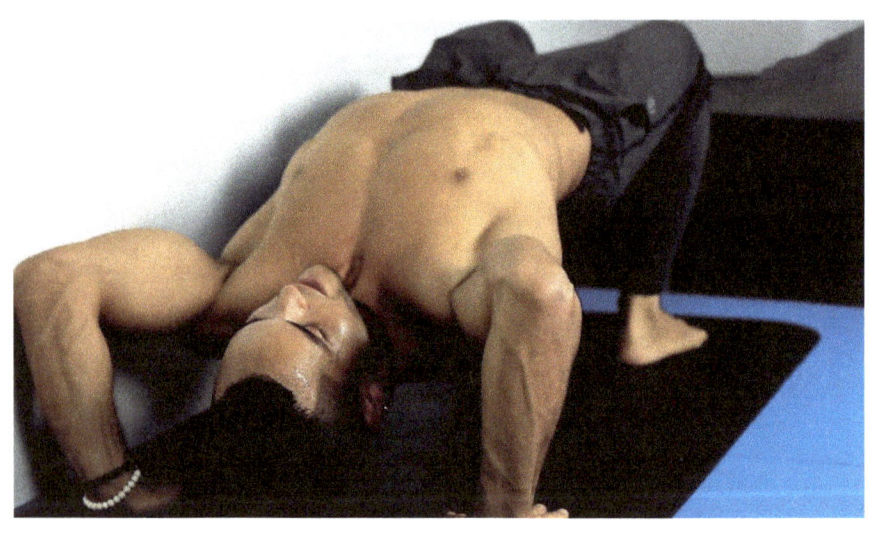

CPSIA information can be obtained
at www.ICGtesting.com
Printed in the USA
BVHW050808110319

542311BV00023B/1382/P